A WORLD OF RECIPES

China

REVISED AND UPDATED

Julie McCulloch

Heinemann Library
Chicago, Illinois

www.heinemannraintree.com
Visit our website to find out more information about Heinemann-Raintree books.

To order:
☎ Phone 888-454-2279
▣ Visit www.heinemannraintree.com to browse our catalog and order online.

Edited by David Andrews and Diyan Leake
Designed by Richard Parker
Illustrated by Nicholas Beresford-Davis
Picture research by Mica Brancic
Printed and bound in China by Leo Paper Products Ltd

13 12 11 10 09
10 9 8 7 6 5 4 3 2 1

New edition ISBN: 978-1-4329-2231-3

The Library of Congress has cataloged the first edition as follows:
McCulloch, Julie, 1973-.
 China/Julie McCulloch.
  p. cm. -- (A world of recipes)
 Includes bibliographical references and index.
 ISBN 1-58810-152-5 (library binding)
      ISBN 978-1-58810-152-5 (HC)
      ISBN 978-1-58810-386-4 (PB)
      Cookery, Chinese—Juvenile literature. [1. Cookery, Chinese. 2. China –Social life and customs.] I. Title.
TX724.5.C M353 2001
641.5951—dc22   00-063275

Acknowledgments
The author and publishers are grateful to the following for permission to reproduce copyright material: Gareth Boden pp. **8–13**, **16–43**; © Capstone Global Library Ltd/MM Studios pp. **14**, **15**; Photolibrary Group pp. **5** (Mauritius/Rafael Macia), **6** (Reso/Charbonneau Charbonneau), **7** (Creatas).

Cover photograph of fried shrimp with vegetables and a bowl of rice reproduced with permission of Getty Images (StockFood Creative/Klaus Arras).

Every effort has been made to contact copyright holders of any material reproduced in this book. Any omissions will be rectified in subsequent printings if notice is given to the publisher.

All the Internet addresses (URLs) given in this book were valid at the time of going to press. However, due to the dynamic nature of the Internet, some addresses may have changed, or sites may have changed or ceased to exist since publication. While the author and Publishers regret any inconvenience this may cause readers, no responsibility for any such changes can be accepted by either the author or the Publishers.

Contents

Some words are shown in bold, **like this**. You can find out what they mean by looking in the glossary.

China

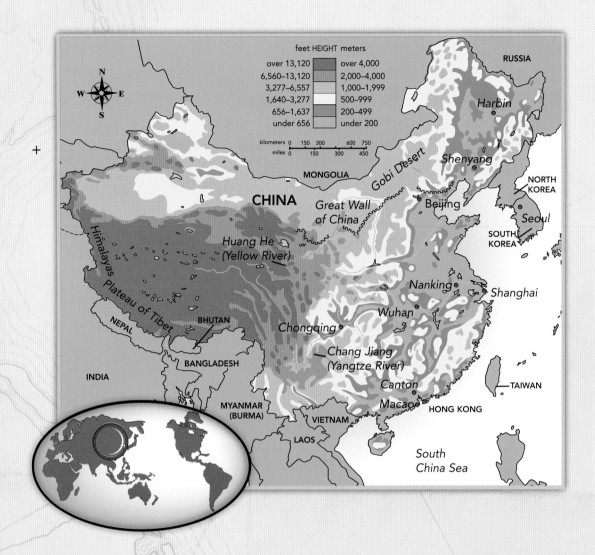

More people live in the People's Republic of China than in any other country. This great nation rose up from a land that is as varied as its people.

China is in eastern Asia, beside the Pacific Ocean. To the southwest stand the Himalayas, the world's highest mountains. The Gobi Desert lies in the middle of China. In the east, flatter land is used for farming.

The mountains have a cold climate with snow all year. Northern China is also cold. Rain forests grow in the south. In winter, monsoon winds blow from the north, causing cold, dry weather. In summer, monsoons blow in from the ocean. This causes warm weather with heavy rain.

In the past

China is a civilization with thousands of years of written history. The Chinese invented paper. Books were written using calligraphy, an artistic style of ink writing. Later, printing methods were invented. Many ancient records exist about Chinese life.

For centuries, emperors ruled China. They lived in a palace called the Forbidden City, which was built of marble and **tropical** wood. It had over a thousand buildings inside moats and walls. Emperors also had stone walls built along the country's northern border. They wanted to keep out tribes, including the Mongols. Parts of this defense system, called the Great Wall, still stand.

China traded with the west (Europe) along a route called the Silk Road. The Buddhist religion entered from India along this route. Silk, cotton, and porcelain were important Chinese trade goods. For many years, only the Chinese knew the secret of how to spin silk threads from the cocoon of the silk worm. This made silk fabric very expensive.

⬆ Statues of lions stand in front of the Forbidden City.

Special times in China

Chinese people continue to honor traditions. They use their own calendar. Their **zodiac** has 12 years represented by animals. Maybe you were born in the year of the snake or the tiger! On New Year's Day, everyone celebrates their birthday, no matter when they were born. Firecrackers are lit and lion dancers perform in the streets.

Chinese Food

The growth of Chinese civilization depended upon two grains: millet and rice. About 7,000 years ago, millet was grown in the north, by the Yellow River. Villages were built where millet could be grown. Rice was first planted in the wetter climate of the south. As more rice was grown, more people could live in China. Today, different kinds of rice are planted in both southern and northern China.

Around the country

Cooking varies among regions because of differences in climate and local traditions. There are eight kinds of Chinese cooking. They are called the Eight Great Traditions. A common saying about Chinese cooking is "East is sweet, South is salty, West is sour, North is spicy."

↑ These people are planting rice in the Chinese province of Yunnan.

Chinese meals

Chinese food is usually prepared in bite-size pieces and eaten using chopsticks. Each person is given a bowl of rice. The other food is placed in the middle of the table for everyone to share. Usually, rice is eaten every day. It might be served at breakfast as a porridge. For lunch and dinner, it is often steamed. In a traditional greeting, people ask, "Have you had your rice today?"

Red meat is eaten less often than fish or chicken. **Vegetarian** dishes include mushrooms, bean sprouts, and leafy vegetables such as bok choy. **Stir-frying**, a method of **frying** vegetables in a pan, has been common since the Tang Dynasty (618–907 CE). Tofu is sometimes served in a stir-fry instead of meat. It is made from soybeans and is high in **protein**.

Festival foods

Red is the color of happiness in China. Red foods are served at weddings and on New Year's Day. Other foods with special meanings are also served on New Year's Day. A whole chicken means family togetherness. Noodles mean long life, so it is bad luck to cut them. Fish served with the head and tail left on means a good beginning and good ending to the year.

↑ Mooncakes like these are eaten to celebrate the harvest festival in China.

Ingredients

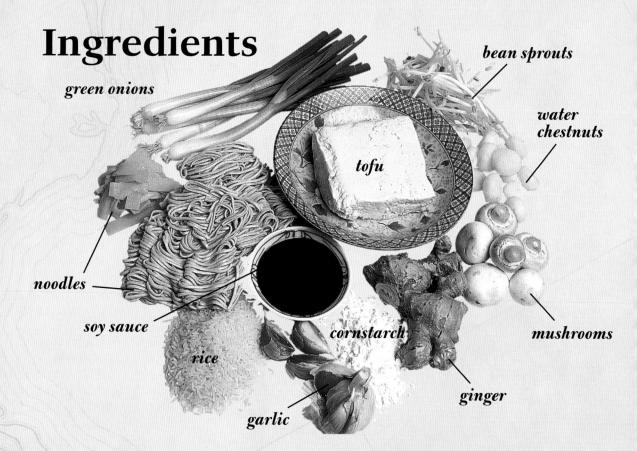

green onions

bean sprouts

water chestnuts

tofu

noodles

soy sauce

rice

garlic

cornstarch

ginger

mushrooms

Chinese cooking uses quite simple ingredients—fresh vegetables, fish, or meat, with a small amount of sauce to bring out their flavor.

Cornstarch

Cornstarch is used in China to thicken sauces. It is often used as part of a sauce called a marinade, as it helps the sauce coat the food. Cornstarch is easy to buy.

Garlic

Garlic is used in many Chinese dishes. You can find garlic in the vegetable section of most supermarkets.

Ginger

Fresh ginger is used in many Chinese dishes, usually **peeled** and **grated**, or finely **chopped**. Ginger is readily available in supermarkets. It is much better to use fresh rather than dried ginger, as its flavor is stronger.

Noodles

There are many different types of noodles in China. Some are made from wheat and egg, some from rice, and some from ground-up beans. The recipes in this book suggest using dried wheat and egg noodles. You should find these noodles, usually just called "egg noodles," in packages in most supermarkets.

Oil

Chinese food is often cooked in sesame oil, made from sesame seeds. If you cannot find any, use vegetable oil instead for these recipes.

Rice

Rice is served with many Chinese dishes. It comes in two main types—short grain and long grain. Chinese people use long-grain rice for most of their dishes.

Soy sauce

Soy sauce is made from soybeans, flour, salt, and water. It is very salty, so you do not need to add any extra salt to your food if it contains soy sauce. You can find soy sauce in most supermarkets.

Tofu

Tofu is made from pulped soybeans. It is called *doufu* in Chinese, but is called tofu in most countries. You can find tofu in most supermarkets.

Vegetables

Chinese cooking uses lots of fresh vegetables, some of which are more familiar outside China than others. The main vegetables used in the recipes in this book are bamboo shoots, bean sprouts, mushrooms, green onions, and water chestnuts. It is easy to buy fresh mushrooms, green onions, and bean sprouts, but you may need to buy canned bamboo shoots and water chestnuts.

Before You Start

Which recipe should I try?

The recipes you choose to make depend on many things. Some recipes make a good main course, while others are better as starters. Some are easy, others are more difficult.

The top right-hand page of each recipe has information that can help you. It tells you how long each recipe will take and how many people it serves. You can multiply or divide the quantities if you want to cook for more or fewer people. This section also shows how difficult each dish is to make: the recipes are easy (*), medium (**), or difficult (***) to cook. The symbols in the corner can help you quickly find certain recipes. Here is a key that will help you.

 Healthy choice: These recipes are healthy to eat.

 Quick and easy: These recipes are quick and easy to make.

 Sweet treat: These recipes make a good dessert or sweet snack.

This symbol ⚠ is a sign of a dangerous step in a recipe. For these steps, be extra careful or ask an adult to help.

Kitchen rules

There are a few basic rules you should always follow when you cook:

- Ask an adult if you can use the kitchen.
- Wash your hands before you start.
- Wear an apron to protect your clothes. Tie back long hair.
- Be very careful when using sharp knives.
- Never leave pan handles sticking out—it could be dangerous if you bump into them.
- Always wear oven mitts to lift things in and out of the oven.
- Wash fruits and vegetables before you use them.

Quantities and measurements

Ingredients for recipes can be measured in two different ways. Imperial measurements use cups, pounds, ounces, and fluid ounces. Metric measurements use grams, liters, and milliliters. In the recipes in this book you will see the following abbreviations:

tbsp = tablespoons   oz. = ounces   cm = centimeters
tsp = teaspoons   g = grams   ml = milliliters
lbs = pounds   in. = inches

Utensils

To cook the recipes in this book, you will need these utensils, as well as kitchen essentials, such as forks, spoons, plates, and bowls.

- Chopping board
- **Colander** or sieve
- Double boiler
- Food processor or blender
- Frying pan
- Grater
- Heatproof bowl
- Kitchen scale
- Large, flat, ovenproof dish
- Measuring cup (for liquids)
- Measuring cups (for dry ingredients) and measuring spoons
- Saucepan with lid
- Sharp knife
- Steamer
- Whisk
- **Wok** (if you don't have a wok, you can use a large frying pan instead)
- Wooden spoon

Mushroom and Water Chestnut Soup

In China, soup is often served between courses. You could also eat this light soup as a starter or for lunch.

What you need

1 onion
1½ cups mushrooms
⅓ cup canned water chestnuts
⅓ cup canned bamboo shoots
2 green onions
2 cups water
1 vegetable stock cube
1 tbsp soy sauce

What you do

1 **Peel** the onion and finely **chop** it.

2 **Slice** the mushrooms.

3 **Drain** the liquid from the canned water chestnuts and bamboo shoots.

4 Cut the tops and bottoms off the green onions and finely chop them.

5 Put the water into a saucepan and bring it to a **boil**. Crumble the stock cube into the water and stir until it **dissolves**. Reduce the heat to a **simmer**.

6 Add the chopped onion and soy sauce to the stock. Simmer it for 10 minutes.

7 Add the mushrooms, water chestnuts, and bamboo shoots. Simmer the soup for another five minutes.

8 Carefully take the soup off the heat. Stir in the chopped green onions.

MUSHROOMS

Over 300 different kinds of mushroom are grown in China! You could try experimenting with different types of mushroom in this dish. Oyster mushrooms and shiitake mushrooms are some of the Chinese mushrooms you might be able to find in your local farmers' market or supermarket.

shiitake mushrooms

oyster mushrooms

Steamed Tofu with Egg

Tofu originated in ancient China. It is made by separating soy milk into curds, which are then pressed into blocks. Tofu has very little flavor or smell on its own, so it can be used either in savory or sweet dishes, and it is often seasoned or **marinated** to suit the dish. It is very nutritious and is a good source of **protein**, iron, and calcium.

What you need

2 eggs
½ tbsp soy sauce
1 tsp sesame oil
1 tsp cornstarch
½ tsp salt
¼ tsp pepper
10½ oz. tofu
1 green onion

What you do

1. **Beat** the eggs in a medium-sized bowl.

2. Add the soy sauce, oil, cornstarch, salt, and pepper to the egg and beat all these ingredients together. Use a spoon to work any cornstarch lumps against the side of the bowl to make a smooth mixture.

3. Roughly **chop** the tofu into chunks.

4 Add the tofu to the egg mixture and combine well.

5 Spoon the mixture into heat-proof serving dishes.

⚠ **6** Place the dishes inside a steamer and steam for 10 minutes.

7 While the tofu is steaming, chop the green onion into small pieces.

8 Scatter the green onion pieces over the steamed tofu and serve.

Shrimp with Ginger Sauce

This dish combines lots of typical Chinese flavors—seafood, ginger, soy sauce, and vinegar. You need to allow 30 minutes for the shrimp to **marinate** in the sauce before you cook them. If possible, use large shrimp, such as tiger shrimp. You can use frozen shrimp, but **defrost** them completely by moving them from the freezer to the refrigerator at least 12 hours before using them.

What You need

A small piece of fresh ginger (about 1 in. long)

1 tbsp soy sauce

1 tbsp vegetable oil

1 tbsp wine vinegar (red or white)

8 oz. cooked and peeled shrimp

A few sprigs of fresh parsley

What You do

1 **Peel** the skin from the ginger and **grate** or finely **chop** it.

2 Mix together the soy sauce, oil, wine vinegar, and chopped ginger in an ovenproof dish.

3 Add the shrimp, stirring them into the mixture so that they are well coated.

4 Leave the shrimp to marinate for 30 minutes.

5 While the shrimp are marinating, chop the parsley.

6 When the shrimp have marinated, turn the broiler on to a medium setting. Put the dish of marinated shrimp under the broiler.

7 **Broil** the shrimp for five minutes, stirring them occasionally.

8 Put the shrimp onto plates, and sprinkle the parsley over them.

Chinese Fish Cakes

Fish cakes (or fish balls, as they are sometimes called) are very popular in China. Some can be **fried**, as shown here, while others are **boiled** in water or stock. You could serve them with rice (see page 19) or noodles (see page 26). If you are using frozen fish fillets, make sure you **defrost** them completely by moving them from the freezer to the refrigerator at least 12 hours before you want to use them.

What you need

- 2 fish fillets
- 2 green onions
- 1 clove garlic
- 1 tsp sugar
- 1 tsp soy sauce
- 2 tbsp vegetable oil
- 2 tbsp cornstarch

What you do

1. Put the fish fillets into a food processor or blender. **Blend** them on a medium setting until they are in tiny pieces.

2. Cut the tops and bottoms off the green onions and finely **chop** them.

3. **Peel** the skin from the garlic clove and finely chop it.

4. Put the fish, green onions, and garlic into a bowl. Add the sugar, soy sauce, and half the oil.

5. Using your fingers, mix everything together. Add about half the cornstarch to bind the mixture together.

6. Sprinkle the rest of the cornstarch onto a chopping board or work surface. Tip the fish cake mixture onto it and divide it into four pieces.

7. Gently shape each piece into a circle, coating the outside in cornstarch.

8 Heat the rest of the oil in a nonstick frying pan over medium heat. Add the fish cakes and fry them for about 10 minutes, turning them occasionally to cook both sides.

9 Serve the fish cakes hot or cold.

PLAIN BOILED RICE

Many Chinese dishes are served with rice. This recipe makes enough plain boiled rice for two people (see also page 36).

1 Put 1 cup of rice into a saucepan.

2 Add 2 cups of water.

3 Bring to a boil, then **simmer** for 20 minutes, stirring occasionally, until the rice has soaked up all the water.

Stir-Fried Fish with Mushrooms and Cucumber

You could use fish such as Pacific cod, tilapia, or red snapper in this recipe. If you are using frozen fish fillets, **defrost** them by moving them from the freezer to the refrigerator at least 12 hours before using them. Serve with plain boiled rice (see page 19).

What You need

2 fish fillets
1 tbsp soy sauce
2 tsp cornstarch
1 small cucumber
½ cup mushrooms
1 clove of garlic
A small piece of fresh
    ginger (about
    1 in. long)
½ cup water
2 tbsp vegetable oil
1 vegetable stock
    cube

What You do

1 Cut the fish fillets into pieces.

2 Mix together the soy sauce and the cornstarch in a bowl. Add the fish pieces, and leave them to **marinate** for about an hour.

3 While the fish is marinating, thinly **slice** the cucumber and mushrooms.

4 **Peel** the garlic and finely **chop** it.

5 Peel the ginger and **grate** or finely chop it.

6 Put half a cup (150ml) of water into a saucepan and bring it to a **boil**. Crumble the stock cube into the water and stir until it **dissolves**. Put the stock to one side.

7 When the fish has marinated, heat the oil in a **wok** or frying pan over medium heat. Carefully put the fish pieces and the marinade into the wok.

8 Add the sliced mushrooms, cucumber pieces, garlic, and ginger to the wok. **Stir-fry** for two minutes.

9 Add the vegetable stock. Reduce the heat, cook for 10 minutes, then serve.

Lemon Chicken Stir-Fry

To make this dish, the chicken needs to be left to **marinate** in the lemon juice and soy sauce, so that it absorbs all their flavors. Try serving it with plain boiled rice (see page 19).

What you need

2 boneless chicken breasts
4 tbsp lemon juice
1 tbsp soy sauce
2 tsp cornstarch
1 clove of garlic
1 tbsp vegetable oil
⅓ cup canned water chestnuts
¼ cup canned bamboo shoots

What you do

1 Take any skin off the chicken breasts and **slice** them.

2 Mix together the soy sauce, the cornstarch, and 2 tbsp of the lemon juice in a bowl. Add the chicken, turning it several times so it is well covered with the mixture.

3 Marinate the chicken for an hour, turning it occasionally.

4 While the chicken is marinating, **peel** the skin from the garlic and finely **chop** it.

5 When the chicken has marinated, heat the oil in a **wok** or frying pan over medium heat. Add the chopped garlic, the chicken, and the marinade, and **stir-fry** for seven minutes.

6 Add the water chestnuts, bamboo shoots, and the rest of the lemon juice. Stir-fry for three minutes more, then serve.

VEGETARIAN VERSION
You could try making a **vegetarian** version of this dish by replacing the chicken with vegetables such as mushrooms or snow peas.

Honey Chicken

Honey or sugar are regularly used in savory Chinese dishes. Chinese cooks feel that a small amount of sweet flavor helps balance the savory or salty ingredients in a dish. Try serving this with plain boiled rice (see page 19).

What you need

A small piece of fresh ginger (about 1 in. long)

2 boneless chicken breasts

2 tbsp soy sauce

¼ cup water

2 tbsp honey

1 tbsp vegetable oil

2 green onions

What you do

1 **Peel** the skin from the ginger and **grate** or finely **chop** it.

2 Take any skin off the chicken breasts and **slice** them.

3 In a bowl, mix together the soy sauce, water, honey, and ginger.

4 Heat the oil in a **wok** or frying pan over medium heat. Add the chicken slices.

5 **Fry** the chicken slices for about five minutes, turning them occasionally.

6 Carefully pour the soy sauce mixture into the wok.

7 Bring the liquid in the pan to a **boil**, put the lid on, and let it **simmer** for 10 minutes.

8 Cut the tops and bottoms off the green onions and finely chop them.

9 Stir the green onions into the chicken mixture, then serve.

CHINESE SUGAR

Chinese cooks use two main types of sugar: brown slab sugar and rock candy. Brown slab sugar is pressed into hard, flat slabs and sold in pieces about 6 in. (15 cm) long. Rock candy is a pale honey color and sold in lumps that look like crystals. You might find some in Asian grocery stores.

Noodles with Ground Pork

This dish is called *mayi hshang shu* in Chinese, which means "ants climbing a tree." The ground pork is thought to look like ants climbing a tree when it is added to the noodles!

What you need

4½ oz. fine egg
   noodles (see page 27)
A small piece of fresh
   ginger (about
   1 in. long)
1 clove of garlic
1 cup water
1 vegetable stock cube
1 tbsp vegetable oil
8 oz. ground pork
1 tbsp soy sauce
2 tsp sugar
2 green onions

What you do

1 Put the noodles into a large bowl. Pour over enough warm water to cover them, and leave them to soak for 15 minutes.

2 **Peel** the ginger and **grate** or finely **chop** it.

3 Peel the garlic and finely chop it.

4 Put the water into a saucepan and bring it to a **boil**. Crumble the stock cube into the water and stir until it **dissolves**. **Cover** the pan and put the stock to one side.

 5 Heat the oil in a **wok** or frying pan over medium heat. Add the ground pork and **stir-fry** for five minutes, until the meat starts to get brown.

6 Add the ginger, garlic, soy sauce, sugar, and vegetable stock to the wok.

7 Carefully **drain** the noodles and stir them into the mixture in the wok. Reduce the heat and **simmer** the mixture for about 15 minutes, until most of the liquid has gone.

8 Cut the tops and bottoms off the green onions and finely chop them.

9 Spoon the pork and noodle mixture onto plates, and sprinkle the spring onions over the top.

NOODLES

Egg noodles are made in different sizes—fine, medium, and thick. They are sold in packages that tell you what size they are. Fine noodles are best for this dish, as they mix well with the ground pork. They are sometimes called thread noodles.

Vegetable Chow Mein

This is a very simple noodle and vegetable dish. Medium egg noodles are the best (see page 27).

What you need

1 cup mushrooms
½ cup snow peas
2 tbsp water
5 oz. medium egg noodles
1 tbsp vegetable oil
½ cup canned bamboo shoots
2½ tbsp soy sauce

What you do

1 **Slice** the mushrooms.

2 Cut the tops and bottoms off the snow peas.

3 Pour the water into a pan and bring it to a **boil**. Add the noodles and boil them for about three minutes, until they are just beginning to get soft.

4 Carefully tip the noodles into a **colander**, and rinse them in cold water.

5 **Drain** the water from the bamboo shoots by emptying them into a sieve or colander.

6 Heat the oil in a **wok** or frying pan. Add the sliced mushrooms, snow peas, and bamboo shoots, then **stir-fry** for four minutes.

Ready to eat: 20 minutes. Difficulty: **. Serves 2.

 **7** Add the drained noodles and soy sauce, stir-fry for about five minutes (until the noodles are hot), and then serve.

NOODLES TO GO
Tasty noodle dishes are served from food stalls all over China. They are called *xiao chi*, which means "small eats," and are eaten as snacks or quick meals.

Tofu Stir-Fry

Tofu tastes quite **bland** on its own, so it is usually cooked with other ingredients that add flavor. In this dish, it is **fried** with enough chili powder to give it flavor, without making the dish too hot and spicy. If you don't like chili, just leave it out.

What you need

1 onion

A small piece of fresh ginger (about 1 in. long)

1 tbsp vegetable oil

3½ oz. tofu

1 tsp chili powder (optional)

Several leaves of bok choy or other greens (see page 31)

1 tbsp soy sauce

What you do

1 **Peel** the skin from the onion and finely **chop** it.

2 Peel the skin from the ginger and **grate** or finely chop it.

3 Cut the tofu into cubes about 1 in. (2 cm) across.

4 Heat the oil in a **wok** or frying pan over medium heat. Add the cubed tofu, chopped ginger, and chili powder (if using), and fry for about 10 minutes, until the tofu is golden brown.

5 Add the chopped onion to the wok and **stir-fry** for three minutes.

6 Cut the bok choy leaves into bite-sized pieces. Add them and the soy sauce to the wok. Stir-fry for two minutes, until the bok choy leaves are just beginning to droop, then serve.

BOK CHOY

Bok choy is a type of Chinese cabbage. It has long, white stems and green leaves. You can usually find bok choy in Asian grocery stores and sometimes in supermarkets. If you cannot find bok choy, you can replace it with fresh spinach in this dish.

Celery and Shrimp Salad

This salad can be served on its own as or a side dish.

What you need

2 stalks of celery

2 green onions

A small piece of fresh
  ginger (about
  1 in. long)

1 cup bean sprouts

2 oz. cooked peeled
  shrimp (**thawed** if
  frozen)

1 tbsp soy sauce

1 tbsp wine vinegar
  (red or white)

1 tbsp vegetable oil

What you do

 Carefully **slice** the celery stalks using a sharp knife.

2 Cut the tops and bottoms off the green onions and slice them.

3 **Peel** the skin from the ginger and **grate** or finely **chop** it.

4 Wash the bean sprouts by putting them into a sieve or **colander** and rinsing them with cold water.

5 Put the chopped celery, green onion, ginger, bean sprouts, and shrimp into a salad bowl.

6 Mix together the soy sauce, vinegar, and oil in a small bowl to make a **dressing** for the salad.

7 Pour the dressing over the salad. Mix everything together and serve.

HOW TO USE CHOPSTICKS

Pick up one chopstick, and hold it between your thumb and first two fingers. This chopstick is the one that will move.

Put the second chopstick between your second and third fingers, and behind your thumb. This chopstick stays still. Move the top chopstick up and down with your thumb and first finger so that the tips of the chopsticks meet.

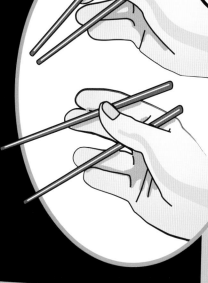

Ginger and Green Onion Noodles

This noodle dish is an ideal accompaniment for some of the main dishes in this book, such as lemon chicken stir-fry (page 22), honey chicken (page 24), and tofu stir-fry (page 30).

What you need

2 green onions

A small piece fresh ginger (about 1 in. long)

4½ oz. medium egg noodles

1 tbsp vegetable oil

1 tbsp soy sauce

What you do

1 Cut the tops and bottoms off the green onions and finely **chop** them.

2 **Peel** the ginger and **grate** or finely chop it.

3 Bring a pan of water to a **boil**. Carefully add the noodles and boil them for about three minutes, until they are just beginning to get soft.

4 Tip the noodles into a **colander** to **drain** them, then put them back into the pan. Reduce the heat to low.

5 Add the chopped green onions, chopped ginger, oil, and soy sauce.

Stir everything together and cook for another two minutes.

GREEN ONIONS

Green onions, also known as scallions, are used in many Chinese dishes. They have a milder flavor than ordinary onions, and they cook very quickly. This makes them ideal for stir-fries and other dishes that need to be cooked quickly. The green stems of the green onions are sometimes shredded or curled into flower shapes to decorate dishes.

Three Rice Dishes

Here are three different ways of cooking rice to accompany your Chinese meal: coconut rice, rice with peas, and egg fried rice. You could also serve plain boiled rice—see the box on page 19 for how to cook this.

What you need

Coconut rice
Ready to eat:
   25 minutes
1 cup rice
2½ cups coconut milk

Rice with peas
Ready to eat:
   25 minutes
1 cup rice
1 cup frozen peas
2 cups water
1 tbsp soy sauce

Egg fried rice
Ready to eat:
   30 minutes
1 cup rice
2 tbsp vegetable oil
2 eggs

What you do

Coconut rice

1 Put the rice into a saucepan and add the coconut milk.

2 Bring to a **boil**, then **cover** the pan and **simmer** for 20 minutes, stirring occasionally.

Rice with peas

1 Put the rice and peas into a saucepan and add the water.

2 Bring to a boil, then cover the pan and simmer for 20 minutes, stirring occasionally.

3 Sprinkle the rice with the soy sauce before serving.

Egg fried rice

1 Cook the rice on its own as described in the recipes on page 36.

2 Crack the eggs into a small bowl. **Beat** them with a fork or a whisk until the yolk and the white are mixed.

3 Heat the oil in a **wok** or nonstrick frying pan over medium heat. Add the beaten eggs and **fry** them, stirring all the time, for about four minutes.

4 Add the cooked rice to the frying pan and mix well with the egg.

egg fried rice

rice with peas

coconut rice

Sweet Chestnut Balls

Chestnuts have been used in Chinese cooking for thousands of years. These sweet chestnut balls are eaten in China as a dessert or a snack.

What you need

- 1½ cups canned chestnuts
- 3 tbsp honey
- ⅓ cup powdered sugar
- 1 tsp cinnamon

What you do

1. If the chestnuts are in liquid in the can, **drain** them by pouring the chestnuts into a **colander** or sieve and patting them dry with paper towels.

2. Put the chestnuts and the honey into a food processor or blender. **Blend** together on the highest setting.

3. Put the powdered sugar and cinnamon into a bowl and mix them together with a spoon.

4. Using your fingers, take a little of the chestnut and honey paste out of the food processor or blender. Roll it into a ball.

5. Cover the ball in sugar and cinnamon by rolling it in the mixture in the bowl.

6 Repeat steps 4 and 5 with the rest of the chestnut and honey paste.

7 Serve the sweet chestnut balls right away, or keep them in the refrigerator until you are ready to eat them.

ROAST CHESTNUTS
Roast chestnuts are served all over China. In the fall, chestnut sellers set up stalls on the streets of many Chinese cities, where they roast chestnuts over charcoal.

Chocolate Lychees

Lychees are a **tropical** fruit. Originally, they came from southern China, but now people grow them in many tropical countries. They have a very sweet taste and a texture a bit like jelly. If you are using fresh lychees, you will need to **peel** them, so add about 10 minutes to the "Ready to eat" time.

You can melt the chocolate in a heatproof bowl that fits on top of your saucepan or in a microwave oven in a non-metallic, microwave-proof bowl.

What you need

3 oz. plain chocolate

1 cup canned or fresh lychees

What you do

1 Break the chocolate into pieces and put them into the bowl.

2 If you are using a microwave oven, cook the chocolate on medium power for one minute and then stir until melted. Continue on from step 7.

3 If you are using a stove top, put 2 cups (400ml) of water into the saucepan. Heat the water over medium heat until it is just bubbling at the edges, but not **boiling**. Reduce the heat to low.

4 Put the bowl of chocolate on top of the pan without letting it touch the hot water. Leave until the chocolate melts (probably about five minutes).

Ready to eat: 1 hour 25 minutes (including 1 hour to chill). Difficulty: **.
Serves 2.

5 While the chocolate is melting, if you are using canned lychees, **drain** them by pouring them into a sieve or **colander**. Pat them dry with paper towels.

 6 Turn off the heat on the stove top. Using oven mitts, take the bowl of melted chocolate from the top of the pan.

7 Pick up a lychee and dip one half of it into the melted chocolate. Put the lychee onto a sheet of wax paper. (Use a toothpick to help pick up the lychee if you need to.)

8 Repeat step 7 with all the lychees.

9 Put the chocolate-coated lychees to **chill** in the refrigerator

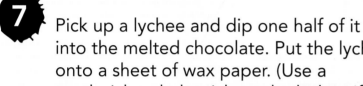

Orange Tea

Chinese people have grown and drunk tea for thousands of years. This recipe suggests using oranges to make a sweet tea that is served at the end of a meal. You could try grapefruit or canned pineapple. Have fun experimenting!

What you need

2 oranges
1 tbsp cornstarch
¼ cup sugar
2 cups water

What you do

1 **Peel** the oranges, then **chop** them into small pieces.

2 Put the cornstarch and sugar into a saucepan and add the water.

 3 Put the saucepan over medium heat and bring the mixture to a **boil**, stirring all the time.

4 Add the orange pieces.

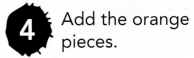 5 Reduce the heat to medium and **simmer** the tea for another five minutes. Serve and drink carefully—it will be hot!

DIFFERENT TEAS

Many different types of tea are produced in China. Different areas of the country produce different flavor teas. Some of the Chinese teas you might be able to find in supermarkets include:

- Oolong: a smooth, fruity, slightly spicy tea
- Lapsang souchong: a strongly flavored tea, in which the leaves are smoked to give a smoky smell and flavor
- Gunpowder: a tea made from grayish tea leaves.

Further Information

Here are some places to find out more about life in China and Chinese cooking.

Books

Bojang, Ali Brownlie. *China* (*Destination Detectives*). Chicago: Raintree, 2006.

Goodman, Polly. *Food in China* (*Food Around the World*). New York: PowerKids, 2008.

Lee, Frances. *The Young Chef's Chinese Cookbook* (*I'm the Chef*). New York: Crabtree, 2007.

Locricchio, Matthew. *The Second International Cookbook for Kids*. Tarrytown, N.Y.: Marshall Cavendish, 2008.

Sheen, Barbara. *Foods of China* (*A Taste of Culture*). Detroit: KidHaven, 2006.

Yu, Ling. *Cooking the Chinese Way* (*Easy Menu Ethnic Cookbooks*). Minneapolis: Lerner, 2009.

Websites

www.apples4theteacher.com/holidays/chinese-new-year/recipes

http://chinesefood.about.com/od/resourceschinesecooking/a/teachingcooking.htm

http://kids-cooking.suite101.com/article.cfm/chinese_food_recipes_for_kids

www.yumyum.com/rsearch.htm?cat=browse&title=browse&keyword=Chinese

www.globalgourmet.com/destinations/china

Healthy Eating

This diagram shows the types and proportion of food you should eat to stay healthy. Eat plenty of foods from the *grains* group and plenty from the *fruits* and *vegetables* groups. Eat some foods from the *milk* group and the *meat and beans* group. Foods from the *oils* group are not necessary for a healthy diet, so eat these in small amounts or only occasionally.

Many Chinese dishes are served with rice or noodles, which belong to the grains group. In China, people eat some meat and fish, as well as tofu, which is made from soybeans. They also use lots of fresh vegetables, so you can see how healthy Chinese cooking is!

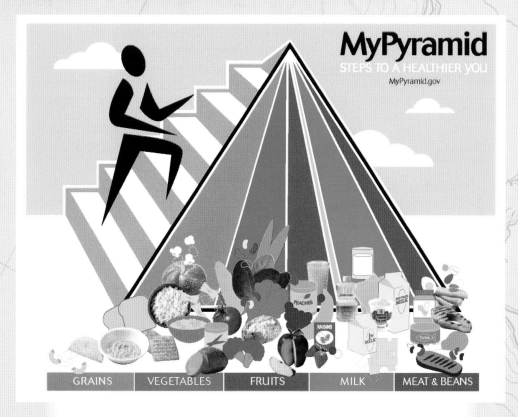

↑ The MyPyramid food pyramid shows the proportion of food from each food group you should eat to achieve a healthy, balanced diet. This takes into account everything you eat, including snacks.

Glossary

beat mix something together strongly using a fork, spoon, or whisk

bland without much flavor

blend mix ingredients together in a blender or food processor

boil cook a liquid on the stove top. Boiling liquid bubbles and steams strongly.

broil cook by being exposed to direct heat

chill put something in the refrigerator to make it cold before serving it

chop cut something into pieces using a knife

colander bowl-shaped container with holes in it, used for draining vegetables and straining

cover put a lid on a pan, or foil over a dish

defrost allow something that is frozen to thaw

dissolve mix something until it disappears into a liquid

drain remove liquid, usually by pouring something into a colander or sieve

dressing oil and vinegar sauce for a salad

fry cook something in oil in a pan

grate break something, such as cheese, into small pieces using a grater

marinate soak something, such as meat or fish, in a mixture called a marinade before cooking, so that it absorbs the taste of the mixture

peel remove the skin of a fruit or vegetable

protein body-building material found in some foods, such as beans, eggs, and meat

simmer cook a liquid on the stove top. Simmering liquid bubbles and steams gently.

slice cut something into thin, flat pieces

stir-fry fry something very quickly in a wok or frying pan, stirring all the time

thaw defrost something that has been frozen

tropical hot, wet climate

vegetarian food that does not contain meat or fish. People who don't eat meat or fish are called vegetarians.

wok round, deep pan used for cooking many Chinese dishes

zodiac system of identifying years with one of twelve animals. Every twelve years, the cycle repeats.

Index